JUST LOOK AT...
FLIGHT

Neil Ardley

Macdonald Educational

Factual Adviser: Kenneth Gatland
Aerospace Consultant

Series Editor: Nicole Lagneau
Editor: Suzanne Greene
Teacher panel: John Allen,
Shimon Levison, Joanne Waterhouse
Designer: Ewing Paddock
Production: Rosemary Bishop
Picture Research: Kathy Lockley

Illustrations
Mike Atkinson 8–9, 10–11B, 20–21, 26–27,
38–39
Ann Baum/Linda Rogers Associates 12–13,
14–15, 16–17
Kuo Kang Chen 32–33, 34–35, 36–37, 40–41
Jeremy Gower/B.L. Kearley Ltd 23, 24–25,
28–29, 30–31
Gary Rees/Linda Rogers Associates 10–11T
Paul Wright back cover 8, 10, 22, 26, 33

How to use this book

Look first in the contents page to see if the subject you want is listed. For instance, if you want to find out about kites, you will find that they are on pages 26 and 27. The word list explains the more difficult terms found in this book. The index will tell you how many times a particular subject is mentioned and whether there is a picture of it.

Flight is one of a series of books on Transport. All the books on this subject have a purple colour band around the cover. If you want to know more about transport, look for other books with a purple band in the **Just Look At** . . . series.

Photographs
Aldus Archive 20
Heather Angel 12, 15
Austin J Brown 23 (Philip Clark), 33,
Barnaby's Picture Library 42
BBC Hulton Picture Library 18, 24
Camera Press front cover
Richard Cooke 34, 35
Daily Telegraph Colour Library 18–19
Rex Features 43B
Freeman 18L
Robert Harding Picture Library 27
Mansell Collection 31
N.A.S.A. 25T
N.H.P.A./Stephen Dalton 15, 17
Popperfoto 21
Royal Aeronautical Society 38
Jerry Young title page

Title page photo: 'Sea Fury' in clouds.

© Macdonald & Co. (Publishers) Ltd

First published in Great Britain in 1984
by Macdonald & Co. (Publishers) Ltd.
London & Sydney.

ISBN 0 356 10184 3
Printed and bound in Great Britain by Purnell & Sons
(Book Production) Ltd., Paulton, near Bristol.

Macdonald & Co. (Publishers) Ltd.
Maxwell House, 74 Worship Street, London EC2A 2EN

Members of BPCC plc. *All rights reserved.*

CONTENTS

UP INTO THE AIR

Even though humans seem to dominate the millions of creatures that live upon the Earth, these creatures have many superior abilities which we may envy, but will never possess. There is one natural power that people have longed to have for thousands of years. We have tried to achieve it in order to feel the excitement and freedom that it brings. This natural power is the power of flight.

Life began on Earth more than a thousand million years ago. It started in the oceans, and slowly spread to the land. Then new types of creatures evolved. They went up into the air, ready to explore every kind of living space. About 300 million years ago, insects became the first creatures to take to the air. Now there is an amazing variety of flying animals in the world's skies.

Over the last 200 years, humans have joined them. Using our intelligence to make up for our lack of wings, we have made some extraordinary flying machines to carry ourselves up into the air. Although these machines do not give us the freedom and grace that a bird has, we have gained the ability to fly much faster than any bird or insect, and also as far and as high as we wish. For the last fifty years, powered flight has affected every aspect of our lives. It has become particularly important in the fields of travel, business and communications.

Powered flight enables this 'flying doctor' to reach patients hundreds of kilometres apart in the Australian outback.

Swallows, hot-air balloons,
hang gliders and a
supersonic airliner illustrate
some of the many different
ways of flying.

Staying Aloft

Everything that flies, whether it is a flying creature or a flying machine, stays up in the air because it can produce a force to hold it there. This force, which is generally called lift, is stronger than the weight of the animal or machine. Therefore, the animal or machine stays in the air and does not fall to the ground or water below.

Lift is produced when wings of any kind move through the air. It is also produced in other ways by balloons, kites and rockets.

Aerofoils

If you were able to cut through a wing, whether it be the wing of a bird or an aeroplane, you would see that the wing is thicker in the middle so that the top surface is curved more than the underneath of the wing. This shape is called an aerofoil, and it is essential to winged flight.

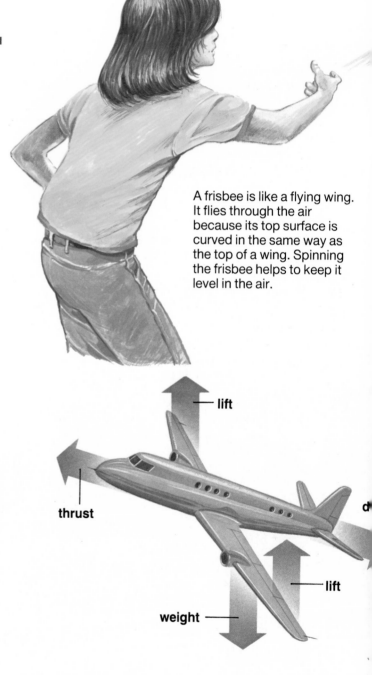

A frisbee is like a flying wing. It flies through the air because its top surface is curved in the same way as the top of a wing. Spinning the frisbee helps to keep it level in the air.

◀ Some kinds of flying duck have to run across the water in order to get up enough speed to take off.

▲ Four forces – lift, weight, thrust and drag – combine to make an aircraft fly through the air.

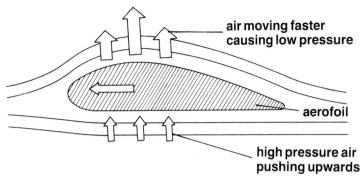

▲ As an aerofoil moves through the air, the air above it moves faster than the air below. This produces a difference in air pressure, which produces lift.

Winged flight

As a wing moves through the air, the air has to move aside faster over the top of the wing than beneath it. The movement lowers the pressure of the air, and the faster-moving air above the wing has less pressure than the slower-moving air beneath. The difference in air pressure makes the air push the wing upwards with a certain amount of force or lift. The faster the wing moves, the greater the lift. This is why an airliner has to speed along a runway to take off and a water bird, such as a duck, has to 'run' over the water to become airborne. Both need to get up to a certain speed for their wings to produce enough lift to carry them into the air. Other birds and flying animals have only to jump into the air or fall from a support to fly. Once in the air, an aircraft uses its engines and birds flap their wings to push air backwards.

This action forces them forwards. Gliders and soaring birds have to descend at a slight angle to keep moving, but they can rise by using winds or air currents.

Balloons, kites and rockets

Balloons fly because they contain either hot air or helium or hydrogen gas. This makes the whole balloon lighter than air and it floats up into the air in the same way as a piece of wood rises in water. The force of the wind pushes kites forwards.

Rockets burn a fuel that produces hot gases, which rush from the exhaust at the base. This action pushes the rocket upwards. Firework rockets fly up into the air until their fuel is finished, while space rockets travel up through the air until they reach space above the atmosphere.

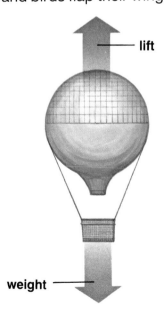

▲ Lift and weight combine to make a balloon float up into the air or sink towards the ground.

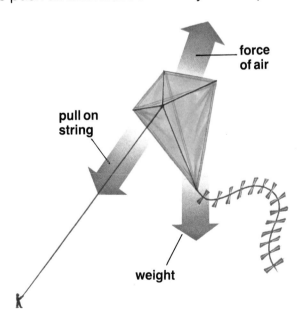

▲ The force of air blowing against a kite is balanced by its weight and the pull on the string to keep it in the air.

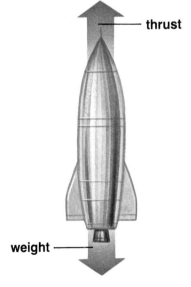

▲ A rocket's engine produces thrust that overcomes the rocket's weight to push it up through the air into space.

Feathers for Flight

Birds are far more at home in the air than any other group of animals. The ability to fly enables them to live throughout the world, travelling great distances, if necessary, to find food and raise their young.

Feather power

The ability to fly is not one that only birds possess, although birds can fly faster, farther and for longer than any other flying creatures. Nor can all birds fly. Penguins use their wings to swim, for example. However, birds have one very important feature that no other animal has: feathers. These vary in number from more than 25,000 for a swan to about 1,000 for a tiny hummingbird.

▲ A hummingbird hovers in front of a flower, feeding on the nectar inside.

▲ A pigeon begins a down-stroke of its wings.

▲ The feathers close together to push the air down and back.

▲ The down-stroke comes to an end.

Kinds of feathers

Feathers give birds their superb powers of flight. They also keep them warm, and give their bodies particular markings that are very important for their survival.

A bird's wing is made of strong feathers called flight feathers. They are attached to the bird's arm and finger bones. There are three main kinds of feathers – primary, secondary and tertiary feathers. The secondary and tertiary feathers are attached to the two short arm bones on the inner half of the wing. These feathers produce lift. The primary feathers are attached to the long finger bones on the outer part of the wing. These feathers can be moved close together or spread apart by the finger bones, which move rather like our fingers. A bird controls its flight with its primary feathers, closing the feathers, spreading them out or twisting them in various ways to fly in any direction. The tail feathers are also used to help the bird turn and change its speed.

Flapping, soaring and hovering

In these ways, birds can power their flight by flapping their wings, or they can soar on outstretched wings. Some can even hover without moving.

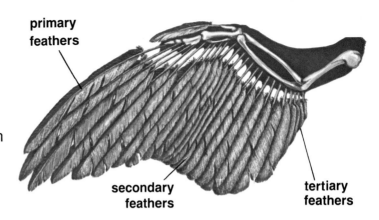

primary feathers

secondary feathers

tertiary feathers

▲ A bird's wing feathers are attached to the bones of its forearm and long finger bones.

They either do this by flying into the wind at the same speed as it blows them back like kestrels or, like the hummingbird, hover by flapping their wings in a fast, complicated pattern that produces lift without movement.

Contour and down feathers

Birds have two other kinds of feathers as well as flight feathers. Contour feathers cover the bird's body, and down feathers are fluffy feathers beneath the contour feathers. Very young birds are covered only with down feathers.

▲ The up-stroke now begins.

▲ The feathers part to allow air to pass through them.

▲ The up-stroke ends and another down-stroke begins.

Birds and Insects

Of all the kinds of animal that can fly, two really have the freedom of the skies. These are birds and insects. While birds hold all the flight records for the animal world, insects such as bees and dragonflies are capable of manoeuvres in the air that make birds look clumsy by comparison.

Birds are not only the fastest fliers of the world, but the swiftest of all animals. The peregrine falcon can reach an astonishing speed of 350 km/hr as it dives upon its prey. In level flight, the speed record is held by the spinetail swift at 170 km/hr. It reaches this speed with the help of its swept-back wings and streamlined body.

Largest birds

A bird's wing muscles must be powerful to enable it to fly. They are large in relation to the size of the bird's body. This gives flying birds, for example, chunky or plump bodies packed with muscle. If a bird is too big, it cannot produce enough power to raise itself into the air. Very large birds like the ostrich are just too heavy to fly. The biggest flying birds are bustards, which are land birds, swans (water birds) and albatrosses (sea birds). They all weigh up to about 18 kilograms. The wandering albatross has the biggest wingspan of all birds. Its wings can measure up to 4 metres across: the width of a medium-sized room.

Long-distance birds

Birds can fly very long distances. After leaving the nest, sooty terns take to the air and do not come down for three to four years! During this time, they eat insects, drink and bathe in rain water, and sleep as they ride on air currents. The greatest distance flown in a year is about 40,000 km by the arctic tern. It migrates from the Antarctic to the Arctic and back every year, covering a distance equal to a flight around the world.

▲ This photograph of a green lacewing fly shows how the insect's wings move as it takes off from a leaf.

▲ Archeopteryx, the earliest known bird, lived about 130 million years ago. Nobody knows how it got off the ground.

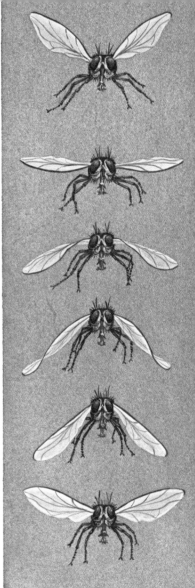

High fliers

The greatest height reached by birds is over 8,000 metres – almost as high as Mount Everest. Mountain birds and migrating swans have been seen at this height.

Flying insects

As they zoom through the air, flying insects such as flies and dragonflies may appear to fly very fast but this is because they are small creatures. Although they may reach as much as 60 km/hr in a burst of speed, no insect can keep up a speed of more than 40 km/hr.

Many flying insects can dart in any direction, twist and turn with ease, and hover without moving in the air. They achieve such control over their flight by moving their wings in very fast and extremely complicated patterns.

▲ A Galapagos hawk soars easily through the air, its wings outstretched to gain lift and keep it aloft.

▲ When insects fly they flap their wings so that the wingtips move in a figure of 8 pattern.

Many insects beat their wings so fast that they give out a buzzing sound. Midges have the fastest wingbeat: up to about 1,000 beats per second!

Migrating insects

Insects take to the air to migrate, as birds do. Painted lady butterflies may fly as much as 6,000 km from Asia or Africa right across Europe to Iceland. In America, monarch butterflies fly the length of the United States or out across the Pacific Ocean to Hawaii. Some even cross the Atlantic Ocean to Europe. However, the butterflies are helped by the fact that they can settle on the sea to rest.

Flying Animals and Plants

Animals have been able to fly for at least 300 million years. This is the age of the oldest known flying creature, a fossil dragonfly found in a coal mine in Britain. Since then, a great variety of flying animals have taken to the air. Today mammals, reptiles, amphibians and even fishes can fly, in addition to birds and insects. The largest animal that ever flew was an extinct kind of flying dinosaur called a pterosaur, which lived in Texas in the United States about 65 million years ago. Its wingspan was 12 metres!

Bats

Apart from birds and insects, the only other animals that fly by flapping or beating their wings are bats. Bats are mammals, and nearly a thousand different kinds live throughout the world.

Bats have wings that are very similar to those of the pterosaurs of long ago, even though they are not related to these extinct animals. Each wing is made of a broad fold of skin that stretches from the bat's long finger bones back to each leg. A bat can move its finger bones and legs to change the shape of the wings so that it can easily twist and turn in the air, even at very low speeds. You can usually see bats at dusk, flitting here and there hunting insects.

Flying fish leap from the water with a twist of the tail and then glide above the waves usually only for a couple of seconds, before falling into the sea again.

Gliding and parachuting animals

Other kinds of flying animals cannot power their flight by flapping wings. In fact, they do not have real wings. Most have folds of skin that they can spread out like wings to support themselves in the air. The 'wings' enable them to glide or parachute through the air. These animals live mostly in forests. They take to the air to jump from tree to tree, usually to find food or escape enemies.

Flying squirrels have large flaps of skin between their legs. The flaps of flying lemurs go up to the chin and tail. To glide, these animals jump into the air and stick out their legs. Squirrels and lemurs are mammals. The flying lizard is a reptile. It has rounded wings made of folds of skin stretched between some rib bones. The bones are tucked into the body but the lizard can glide by extending them to form wings. Flying frogs are amphibians. They have webbed feet that act as parachutes.

This false vampire bat is about to swoop on a mouse. You can clearly see the long finger bones and leg bones to which the wings are attached. ▶

Flying fish

The flying fish escapes its enemies by taking to the air. It swims up to the surface of the sea at about 30 km/hr, and then spreads out its fins to form wings. It beats its tail in the water, increasing its speed to as much as 50 km/hr. Then it glides above the water, usually for a few seconds, although once a flying fish was seen to fly over one kilometre, taking 90 seconds.

Airborne plants

Some plants also make use of flight, though they themselves do not move. Plants have tiny seeds or spores which are so light that the wind carries them far away. Eventually they all fall to the ground. As the wind has separated them they all fall in different places, sometimes very far apart. This means that it is likely that some of the seeds or spores will land on soil which is good for them, and that they will grow into new plants. The dandelion is one of the best-known examples of this type of seed dispersal.

Sycamore seeds are shaped like wings and whirl as they drop. This slows their fall so that the wind blows them some distance from the tree.

FREE AS A BIRD

For centuries, people have tried to fly like birds by strapping home-made wings to their wrists, launching themselves into the air and then bravely flapping their arms. Nobody has ever succeeded, and it's unlikely that anyone ever will. The main reason is that we are not strong enough to raise ourselves into the air, even with the very best wings. People, like ostriches, are just too heavy to fly.

We can solve this problem by using an engine to provide enough power to propel us through the air in an aeroplane. However, there are several other ways in which we can fly without using a source of power. Balloons, gliders and kites can carry people into the air. This kind of unpowered flight depends on the strength and direction of the wind, but it is very exciting and many people enjoy it as a sport. In a hang glider, for example, a person can really fly high in the air, with the freedom and exhilaration of any soaring bird.

Recently, it has even become possible for people to fly by their own efforts. Very light human-powered planes can take to the air. Their pilots use pedals like bicycle pedals to turn a propellor. In 1979, a pedal plane called the Gossamer Albatross made the first human-powered flight across the English Channel, covering a distance of 36 km.

▲ In the Greek myth, Icarus crashes into the sea, as the sun melts the wax fixing his wings. His father, Daedalus, looks on helplessly.

▲ The Marquis de Bacqueville was one of many pioneers who tried to fly with wings attached to their arms. In 1742 he tried to fly over the River Seine in Paris. He crashed on a raft, and broke his legs.

▲ The pedal-powered Gossamer Albatross shortly before taking off on its historic flight across the English Channel in 1979.

The hang glider enables
people to ride winds and air
currents and soar easily
through the air, almost
like a bird. ▶

Lighter than Air

One way in which people can be carried up into the sky has been obvious for many thousands of years. Yet it was not until 1783, just 200 years ago, that it was used for human flight. This method can be seen in any smoking fire. The smoke is carried upwards by the heat of the flames. The reason is that hot air is lighter than cool air, so hot air rises through the cool air around it and it floats above the cool air.

At the beginning of the 1700s, scientists realized that a large balloon full of hot air would be light enough to fly, and perhaps to carry people. The first model hot-air balloon was made of paper and flew in 1709 in Portugal, but a full-scale balloon did not immediately follow. Then, in 1766, the gas known as hydrogen was discovered. It was found to be very light indeed and could lift a balloon. People then experimented with hot air and with hydrogen to build the first balloons.

The first balloons

The year 1783 saw a race to get the first balloon aloft. Some people worked with hot air and others preferred hydrogen. The race took place in France and was won by two brothers, Joseph and Etienne Montgolfier. They built (but did not fly) the first hot-air balloon. The balloon was filled with hot air from fires on the ground and in the base of the balloon. In September 1783, a sheep, duck and cock became the first creatures to go up in a human-made flying machine. Then a month later, a man called François Pilâtre de Rozier went up successfully in a tethered balloon. This was followed by the first free human flight on 21 November 1783, when Pilâtre de Rozier and the Marquis d'Arlandes flew over Paris for 25 minutes and returned safely to the ground. Ten days later, Jacques Charles followed them into the air in a hydrogen balloon which he had invented.

▲ The first aerial crossing of the English Channel was made in 1785 by a hydrogen balloon equipped with oars.

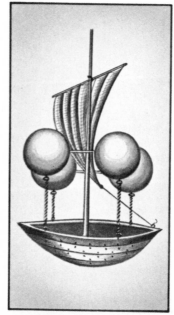

◄ A design for a flying boat made by Francesco de Lana in 1670. The air inside the copper globes was to be pumped out so that the boat would float into the sky like a balloon. The copper globes were very thin and would have collapsed under the pressure of the air outside.

Ships of the air

Balloons were very good at lifting people into the air, but once in the air, the balloon travelled only as far and fast as the wind would allow. So people started thinking of ways to stop the wind blowing a balloon wherever it liked. They wanted to control the balloon's flight. The first idea was to have oars like a boat and to row through the air. Such an airship, as powered balloons came to be called, was rowed over the English Channel in 1785. The journey took two and a half hours but it's very unlikely that the oars made much difference: a gentle wind blew the hydrogen-filled balloon on its way.

The first real airships contained engines that powered propellors to drive the balloon and its cabin through the air. A steam-powered airship first flew in 1852 in France, and the first airship with a petrol engine took to the air in Germany in 1888. From 1900 on, airships became the first flying machines to make fully controlled flights and huge passenger-carrying airships driven by petrol engines began to appear. The balloons in these airships contained hydrogen, as hot air was not light enough. Unfortunately hydrogen burns easily, and airships began to catch fire and explode. After a series of disasters in the 1930s, airships were abandoned, although a few have been made recently, using hot air or helium gas.

▲ In 1937, the German airship Hindenburg caught fire, killing 35 people. The disaster occurred because the airship contained hydrogen gas, which burns easily.

The first hydrogen balloon flew from Paris in August 1783. It landed in a nearby village and was attacked by the villagers who thought it was a monster. ▼

Ballooning Today

Balloons today are used for several purposes. Many are simply flying advertisements. Most of these carry brand names on their sides, but there are some spectacular balloons that are made in the shape of the products they advertise, such as light bulbs, ice-cream cones and even jeans! Balloons may also have a more serious purpose, and many are used to carry automatic instruments high into the upper atmosphere. These are called high-altitude balloons. There they measure conditions and make observations of the land below. This information is sent back in the form of radio signals and can help to make weather forecasts and detect air pollution.

Sports balloons

Flying a balloon is a popular sport. Great pleasure can be found in floating quietly over the countryside, going wherever the wind may lead. Unlike high-altitude balloons, which contain hydrogen or helium, sport balloons use hot air. This is because hydrogen is dangerous and helium expensive.

Getting a hot-air balloon into the sky is quite a complicated task. The huge, round nylon envelope of the balloon is first laid out on the ground, and some air is then either trapped or blown inside it. This air is then heated by sending flames from a large gas burner through the open neck of the envelope. The envelope slowly inflates as the air inside gets warmer. When it is almost ready to rise, the crew scrambles into the basket beneath the envelope and lights the burner above the basket. The balloon then floats up into the sky, lifted by the hot air inside the envelope.

The crew stays in the air by relighting the burner whenever necessary, in order to keep the air inside hot. The crew can pull a cord to open a panel in the envelope. This releases hot air, and is used either when descending, or when deflating the balloon at the end of the flight.

Balloon records

Balloons can fly as high as 50 km above the ground, though not with people aboard. The highest that a balloonist has reached is nearly 38 km. The longest distance flown by a balloon was the first balloon flight across the Pacific Ocean in 1981. The balloon, Double Eagle V, took four days to make its journey of more than 8,000 km from Japan to the United States. These record-breaking balloons are filled with gas, not hot air. Balloonists hope one day to make a balloon flight around the world. Riding the fast-moving high-altitude winds called jet streams, the flight would take about 20 days.

Advertisers make balloons in all sorts of strange shapes in order to promote their products. ▶

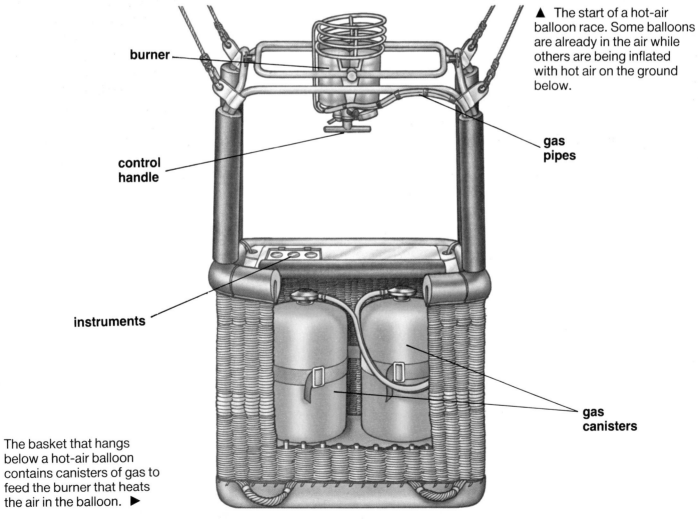

burner

control
handle

instruments

gas
pipes

gas
canisters

▲ The start of a hot-air
balloon race. Some balloons
are already in the air while
others are being inflated
with hot air on the ground
below.

The basket that hangs
below a hot-air balloon
contains canisters of gas to
feed the burner that heats
the air in the balloon. ▶

Gliding

Gliders were the first heavier-than-air aircraft that ever flew. As long ago as 1804, the British engineer Sir George Cayley worked out the basic shape of such an aircraft. He built and flew model gliders with a long body, a central pair of wings and a tail, just like modern aircraft. Yet, it was not until 1849 that Cayley succeeded in making a glider big enough to carry a person. It needed three pairs of wings and even then, an adult was too heavy for it. So the first person to fly in an aircraft that was heavier than air was a ten year old boy. The glider carrying the boy was towed by hand down a hill facing the wind, and he flew a short distance.

Getting up into the air
Unlike a balloon or a powered aircraft, a glider cannot leave the ground and rise into the air on its own. In order to take off it has to be pulled along the ground by a rope attached to an engine, or it may be towed behind an aircraft. The glider is released when its speed through the air is fast enough to enable the wings to support the glider. It then keeps up its speed by gradually sinking, and eventually it has to land. Rising air currents may push the glider higher and make its flight last longer.

Sailplanes
Modern gliders are used mainly for sport, and they are often known as sailplanes. They have very long slender wings that can produce enough lift for flight at slow speeds. After launch, the pilot seeks rising air currents to gain height. These may be winds blowing up the sides of hills, or rising currents of warm air called thermals. Factories and fields or rocks warmed by the sun often have thermals above them. Some types of cloud contain air currents that will cause the glider to soar even higher up into the air.

▲ The first heavier-than-air craft to carry a person aloft was this triplane glider invented by Sir George Cayley. In 1849, a ten year old boy flew a short distance in it.

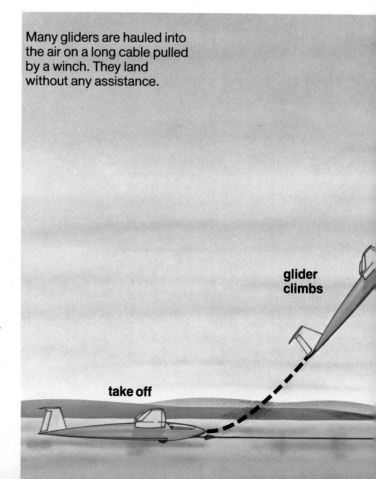

Many gliders are hauled into the air on a long cable pulled by a winch. They land without any assistance.

glider climbs

take off

▲ The German aviation pioneer Otto Lilienthal flying one of his hang gliders in 1896. He crashed to his death in such a glider later the same year.

▲ The first US Space Shuttle Columbia comes into land. The Space Shuttle lands without using its engines and is the world's heaviest and fastest glider. It weighs about 100 tonnes and touches down at a speed of about 350 km/hr.

Controlling the flight

A glider pilot can turn and change speed by operating controls that move flaps on the wings and tail of the glider. By gliding from one rising current to another, a glider can spend hours in the air before returning to its base or being forced to land. The longest glider flight covered more than 1,600 km.

Hang gliders

A daring kind of flying sport called hang gliding has recently become popular. In fact, it was started in the 1890s by a brave German inventor named Otto Lilienthal. He built gliders made of large sets of wings that could be attached to his body. To launch himself into the air, Lilienthal ran down the hills. Then, with his feet dangling in the air, he could shift his weight from side to side or forward and backward to control his flight. In this way, Lilienthal managed to fly as far as 250 metres.

Modern hang gliders are flown in the same way. Take-off is achieved by facing into the wind on a downward slope. The flier then lies horizontally, supported by a frame beneath the large wings. A control bar is held and can be moved to shift the flier's weight and control the flight. The wings of the hang glider are made of cloth, so the glider can be folded up when it is not in use. The triangular wings used in hang gliding are developed from a wing that was specially designed to carry returning spacecraft safely to the ground. It was never used for this purpose, but it has proved very useful in sport.

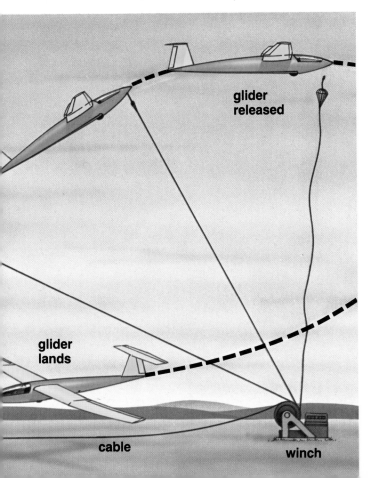

glider released

glider lands

cable

winch

Kites

Kites were the first flying objects to be made by people. Many different kinds of kites have been flown for more than 2,000 years. In order to fly, a kite has to be attached to a line held by someone or something on the ground. It can be controlled to swoop and soar up and down through the air with ease. When towed behind a moving vehicle, a kite can travel through the air like an aircraft.

The first kites were made in China more than two thousand years ago. No-one knows how the kite came to be invented. One possibility is that it developed from banners that streamed in the wind. The Chinese and Japanese built kites that were big enough to carry people up into the air. The explorer Marco Polo saw people-lifting kites when he visited China in the 1200s. So the first human to fly was probably an unknown Chinese person over a thousand years ago. These kites were mainly used to lift people high in the air to spy on an enemy in wartime. The experience was dangerous and unpleasant, and in China kite-flying was also used as a punishment for criminals!

In 1826, the British George Pockock, invented a light-weight carriage drawn by two kites. The famous 'char-volants' were controlled by four lines, and could go in different directions in the same wind.

◀ Many kites, like this one
in the shape of a dragon, are
made to look beautiful as
well as to fly superbly.

Kite-flying today

Today, flying up into the air beneath a kite is done entirely for pleasure. Parascending is a popular sport in which people are fixed to a large kite and towed behind a boat so that they rise into the air. Kites also have serious uses. Carrying spraying equipment, kites can hover low over a field and spray the crops. Low-flying kites are also used to lift radio-controlled cameras into the air to photograph the land below. The pictures can be of great value to archeologists, geologists and surveyors. Kites carrying automatic instruments to high altitudes are used for weather forecasting. These kites can fly as high as 8 km, almost as high as Mount Everest!

How a kite flies

The kite is controlled by the line to which it is attached. It is held at an angle to the wind, or to the air if it is being towed. As the wind or air is pushed downwards, it forces the kite back and up. The kite may also act like a wing and produce lift as the air moves over it. Many kites have wing-like shapes to help give lift. The kite's weight and the pull of the line balance the force of the wind or air so that it stays aloft.

Kites may also have fins or vertical panels, as in box kites. Like the tail of an aircraft, these keep the kite facing into the wind. Flat kites have long tails to do this. Many kites have lines attached to fins or panels to steer them in the air.

Human cargo

People-lifters were developed throughout the 1800s, and in 1901 Samuel Cody, an American showman who lived in Britain, invented the most famous kite system. He used a group of kites to carry a strong line up into the air, and then another kite was used to send an observer up and down the line. Experiments with such people-lifters were important in the development of aircraft, which started being used for observation purposes instead of kites in 1910.

▲ Samuel Cody, an American showman
who lived in Britain, invented this kite to carry
an observer aloft at sea in 1901.

POWERED FLIGHT

All forms of unpowered flight, from the earliest people-lifting kites to the latest kinds of balloons and gliders, depend on the wind. Without it, they can get hardly anywhere and even with a wind, there is little control over a flight. To achieve real control in the air, we need aircraft with powerful engines to drive them in any direction and as high and as far as we wish to fly. Airships had engines, of course, but they were slow-moving and could not change course or height quickly. Wings and a tail driven at speed through the air give plenty of lift to climb with ease, while control surfaces, such as flaps and a rudder enable an aircraft to grip the air and twist and turn in any direction required.

The first aircraft that were heavier than air and able to fly under their own power took to the air in the early years of this century. They used a new kind of engine that was both light and powerful: the petrol engine first invented for the motor car. These early powered aircraft were like a combination of glider and kite systems fitted with propellors, and their flight was hesitant and unreliable.

Improvement upon improvement was made, and flying soon became a safe form of transport. New sources of power in jet engines and even rocket engines have now produced aircraft capable of flight at astonishing speed and height and of astounding size. New ways of using power to fly have resulted in extraordinary flying machines that can hover motionless in the air and even fly backwards.

The US North American Aviation X-15 rocket-powered research plane is the world's fastest aircraft. Its fastest speed was 7927 km per hour, achieved in 1967.

This Vickers Vimy biplane made the first non-stop crossing of the Atlantic Ocean in 1919.

The US Lockheed SR-71 aircraft is the world's fastest jet aircraft and holds the world official air speed record. The record speed of 3530 km per hour was achieved in 1976.

The US Aero Spaceline's Super Guppy is one of the world's biggest aircraft. It can carry nearly 25 tonnes of freight in its enormous 8-metre high hold.

Propellor Pioneers

Propellors were used to power the first aeroplanes or airplanes, as powered winged aircraft are generally called. A propellor is like a fan. As its blades whirl round, they force air backwards and this pushes the aeroplane forward through the air.

First flights

Inventors in the late 1800s and 1900s tried to use steam engines to drive their propellor aircraft. In 1890 the French inventor Clément Ader managed to fly 50 metres in his aeroplane Eole. However, this flight was not controlled. Ader could not even see where he was going as he was seated behind the engine's boiler!

Steam engines were really too heavy for flight, but petrol engines, which were lighter and more powerful, did produce powered flight. After years of experimenting, the American inventors Orville and Wilbur Wright fitted a petrol engine to their aeroplane Flyer 1. On 17 December 1903, Orville Wright first flew Flyer 1 for 12 seconds at a height of about 3 metres. This famous flight, which took place at Kitty Hawk in North Carolina, USA, is considered to be the first powered aeroplane flight.

The first powered flight in Europe was by Alberto Santos-Dumont. In his aeroplane, 14-bis, he flew 220 metres in France on 12 November 1906.

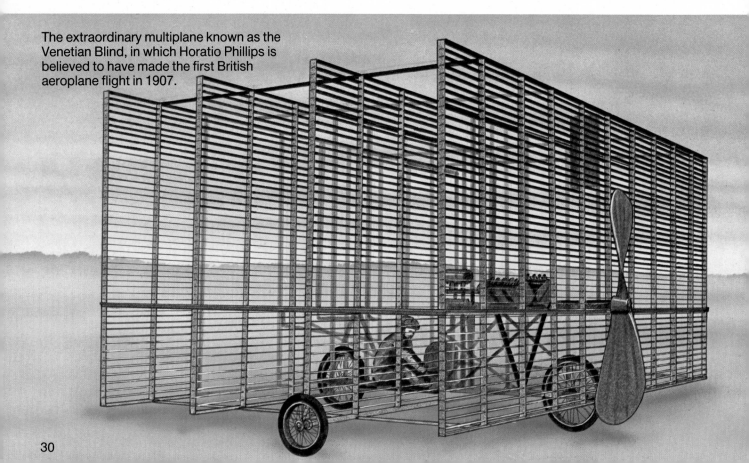

The extraordinary multiplane known as the Venetian Blind, in which Horatio Phillips is believed to have made the first British aeroplane flight in 1907.

Many propellor aircraft are driven by petrol engines similar to those in cars. In early aeroplanes, the cylinders were often arranged around the propellor. The cylinders fired in turn so that the pistons drove a crank that turned the propellor. ▶

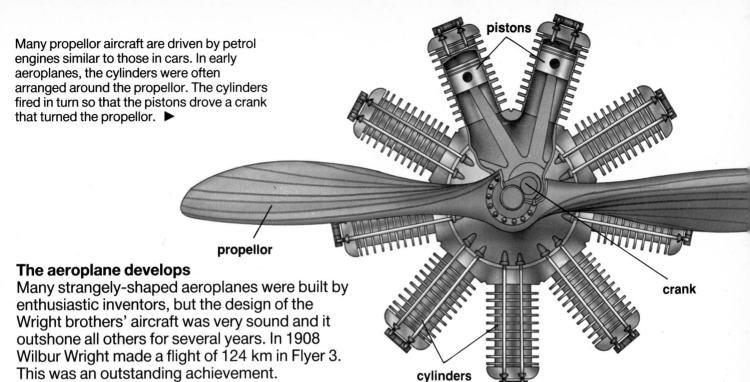

pistons

propellor

crank

cylinders

The aeroplane develops

Many strangely-shaped aeroplanes were built by enthusiastic inventors, but the design of the Wright brothers' aircraft was very sound and it outshone all others for several years. In 1908 Wilbur Wright made a flight of 124 km in Flyer 3. This was an outstanding achievement.

Soon the first airliner, as passenger-carrying aircraft are called, was built. It was made in Russia by Igor Sikorsky in 1913, and was called the Bolshoi, which means 'great' in Russian, because of its size. The Bolshoi was powered by four engines and carried eight passengers in a luxurious cabin.

World War I, from 1914 to 1918, speeded the development of aeroplanes as nations raced to build better fighters and bombers. These aircraft were later used for peaceful purposes. All kinds of designs were tried, with planes sprouting several sets of wings and engines. One of the most spectacular machines to be built was the Italian Caproni Ca 60 flying boat, made in 1919.

The Caproni had nine wings and eight engines plus room for 100 passengers. However, it was very clumsy in the air and only flew twice.

Brave pilots took up many challenges. Some tried to cross the world's oceans in non-stop flights. They demanded the very best aircraft and their feats helped to advance aeroplane design. One epic flight was in 1919 when British pioneers John Alcock and Arthur Brown made the first non-stop Atlantic crossing. The flight, in a Vickers Vimy biplane, took nearly 16½ hours. Another epic flight was the first solo transatlantic flight. This was achieved in 1927 by the American pilot Charles Lindbergh. He flew in a monoplane called Spirit of St Louis, and took just under 33½ hours.

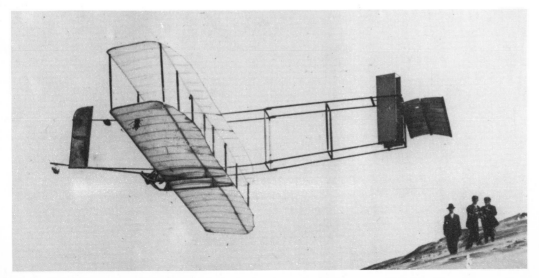

◀ Flyer 1, the first powered aeroplane, making its historic first flight at Kitty Hawk, North Carolina, U.S.A., on 17 December 1903.

From Power to Pleasure

As aircraft design advanced during the 1920s and 1930s, the best aeroplanes were found to be monoplanes driven by one to four engines, according to their size. The most successful aircraft of that time was the twin-engined Douglas DC-3 or Dakota. This American airliner, which carried 21 passengers at 300 km/hr, first appeared in 1935. By 1939, nine out of ten airline passengers were flying in a DC-3.

World War II and after

Aerial warfare was very important in World War II, which lasted from 1939 to 1945. Propellor-driven planes were brought to a peak of performance in the effort to win. Outstanding among many powerful aeroplanes were the Russian Ilyushin II-2 which was known as the Stormovik, the German Junkers Ju-87 dive bomber known as the Stuka, the British Supermarine Spitfire and U.S. and North American Mustang fighters, which could exceed 700 km/hr. There were also large bombers like the British Avro Lancaster and U.S. Boeing Flying Fortress, which had wingspans of 31 metres.

During the war the jet engine arrived, and took over from the propellor as a source of power. No prop-powered plane could outpace a jet fighter, but large propellor-driven aeroplanes were still built. The Lockheed Constellation, an American airliner carrying from 48 to 75 passengers, first appeared in 1946. It became the first airliner to make regular non-stop flights across the Atlantic. However its days were numbered by the development of jet airliners in the 1950s.

The largest propellor aircraft ever built was the U.S. Hughes H-4 Hercules flying boat, completed in 1947. With a wingspan of 97.5 metres, it made one test flight and never flew again.

The Solar Challenger is the world's first solar-powered aircraft and also the lightest powered aircraft. It weighs only 59 kg. ▼

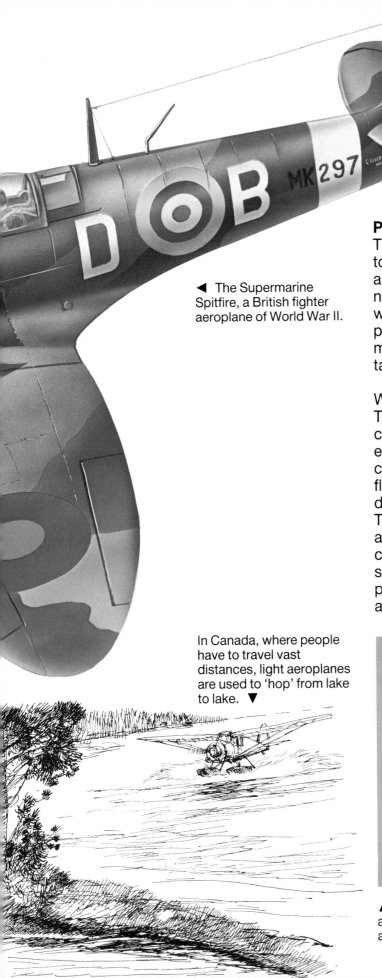

◀ The Supermarine Spitfire, a British fighter aeroplane of World War II.

Propellor planes today

The propellor is still a source of power for flight today. Little propellor planes are used as private aircraft, and small propellor-driven airliners are needed in many places, particularly islands, where runways are short. Sport fliers have added propellors and wheels to hang gliders to produce microlights. These are individual planes that can take off and land almost anywhere.

We now also have planes powered by the Sun. They are called solar-powered planes and are covered in solar cells that change sunlight into electricity. This electricity drives an electric motor connected to a propellor. The Solar Challenger flew across the English Channel in 1981 to demonstrate the arrival of solar-powered flight. This aircraft was built to be as light as possible and could carry only one person because sunlight cannot yet produce very much power. With the safe development of both microlights and solar-powered planes, aircraft should become cheaper, and more people may have their own planes.

In Canada, where people have to travel vast distances, light aeroplanes are used to 'hop' from lake to lake. ▼

▲ A microlight, a miniature propellor aircraft, is a hang glider with a small engine and wheels. Microlights are flown for sport.

Labels on the diagram:

A jet engine

combustion chamber

compressor

burning fuel

turbine

Jet Aircraft

In 1937, a new source of power that would completely change the world of flight was first tested. This source of power was the jet engine. It was invented by the British engineer Sir Frank Whittle.

How a jet engine works

A jet engine sucks in air, raises its pressure in a compressor, and then heats the air with burning fuel in combustion chambers. The heat makes the air expand, forcing it to spin the blades of a turbine which in turn drives the compressor. As the hot air reaches the exhaust, it may be heated even more by burning fuel. The air then rushes from the exhaust at high speed, driving the engine forward. Jet engines give much more power than propellors, and so jet aircraft can fly much faster than propellor-driven aeroplanes.

Jet fighters

By the time jet engines were fitted to aircraft, World War II was being fought, so the first jet planes were fighters. The Germans developed a jet engine soon after Whittle and beat the British to the first jet aircraft. This was the Heinkel He-178, which first flew on 27th August 1939. It could reach a speed of 700 km/hr. The first aircraft to fly with a Whittle jet engine was the British Gloster E28/39, an experimental aircraft. The first operational British jet was the Gloster Meteor. This went into service in 1944, and at speeds of up to about 900 km/hr it could easily outfly any propellor-powered fighters. Today's jet aircraft can fly four times as fast.

The flight deck of an airliner is packed with instruments and controls. The three crew are the pilot, co-pilot and flight engineer. ▶

Bigger and better

After the war, aircraft builders began to use the jet engines for passenger flying. The first jet airliner was the British De Havilland Comet, which made its first passenger flight in 1952. It carried 36 passengers and flew twice as fast as propellor-powered airliners.

Problems

The strain of travelling at such speed and height caused several Comets to crash. The reason was a weakening of the metal called metal fatigue.

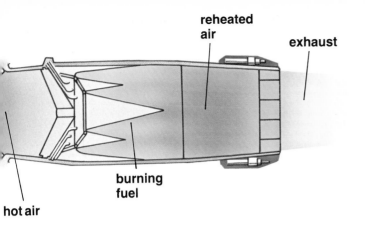

reheated
air

exhaust

burning
fuel

hot air

Jet travel today

Stronger metals and better building methods
have been developed to make jet airliners, and jet
air travel is now very safe.

The great power of the jet engine has now given
us airliners which are huge as well as fast. The
biggest is the U.S. Boeing 747 Jumbo Jet, which
can carry over 600 passengers at nearly
1,000 km/hr. It is so vast that at the front of the
aircraft, there are two decks with a spiral
staircase between them.

▲ The British Sea Harrier fighter can take
off and land vertically by directing the
powerful thrust of its jet engine downwards.
This means it does not need a long runway
from which to take off or land, so it can be
used almost anywhere. When the aeroplane
is in a dive, it can go faster than the speed of
sound.

▲ The German Heinkel He-
178, the world's first jet
aircraft. It first flew on 27
August 1939.

Fast and Slow

For many people, the most beautiful aircraft ever made is the British-French airliner called Concorde. With its long, needle-like body, and elegantly curved wings, it flies more gracefully than any other flying machine in history. Concorde's beauty has a good practical reason: it is designed to cut through the air at enormous speed. It flies at 2,300 km/hr, which is more than twice as fast as the speed at which sound travels. Aircraft that travel faster than the speed of sound are known as supersonic aircraft. Concorde whisks its passengers from France or Britain to the United States in just three hours, whereas an ordinary jet plane would take six or seven hours to do the same journey.

As well as Concorde's expensive fares, there is another price to pay for supersonic flight, and that is noise. The very powerful jet engines of supersonic aircraft are extremely noisy. When an aircraft flies faster than the speed of sound, it makes a loud bang as it passes overhead. Concorde and fast military aircraft go supersonic only over the ocean or areas where there are no people, so that they do not disturb anyone.

Rocket power

A rocket engine works by burning fuels to produce very hot gases. The gases expand violently and force the rocket forwards, giving much greater power than can be achieved with a jet engine.

The first rocket aircraft was a glider fitted with simple powder rockets. It was flown from off the slopes of a mountain by F. Stamer in Germany on 11 June 1928. The first rocket aircraft to take off from level ground was also a converted glider. It was piloted by Fritz von Opel in Germany on 30 September 1929. The most famous early rocket plane was the German Messerschmitt ME-163B Komet, a small fighter which flew in 1941. That year the Komet became the first aircraft to fly faster than 1,000 km/hr. Nowadays, rocket engines are not used in aircraft, but they are always used in spacecraft.

The hovercraft was invented by the British engineer, Sir Christopher Cockerell. A hovercraft directs a powerful blast of air beneath its hull to lift it just above the surface of the water so that it can move easily. The propellors push it forward. ▶

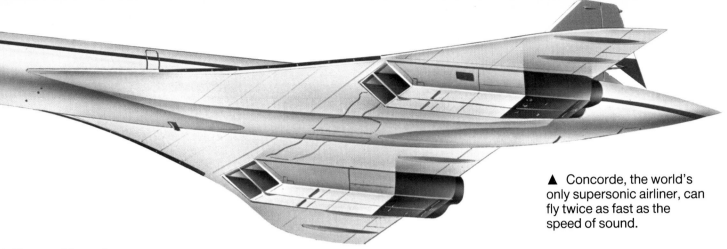

▲ Concorde, the world's only supersonic airliner, can fly twice as fast as the speed of sound.

Record breakers

The first aircraft to go through the sound barrier and fly faster than the speed of sound was rocket-powered. It was the Bell XS-1, an American experimental plane, and in 1947 it became the first supersonic aircraft. The fastest aircraft ever built was the North American X-15, another rocket-powered experimental plane (see page 29). Both of these planes could not take off from the ground, but were released from under a large jet aircraft, high in the air.

Hanging on air

Powerful jet engines have enabled aircraft not only to fly faster and faster, but also to fly slower and slower. During the 1950s, British aircraft designers worked to build an aircraft that could direct the air stream from its jet engine downwards. The aim was to use the engine to support the aircraft in the air, so that it could fly slowly or even hover. The reason for this was that such an aircraft would be able to take off and land either with a very short run or even vertically. This would be very useful because the plane could be used almost anywhere, as it would not need a long runway to take off or land.

The aircraft that was built was called the Hawker Siddeley Harrier (see page 35), and it went into service in 1969. It is a fighter plane, and can be used almost anywhere. Once the Harrier is in the air, the air stream is turned to push the plane forward.

Hovercraft

Hovercraft fly in a similar way. A stream of air is forced by fans beneath the hovercraft, producing a cushion of air that lifts the hovercraft just above the surface of the sea or land. As it is not in contact with surface, the hovercraft can move easily over it, driven forward by propellors.

▲ The German Messerschmitt Me-163B Komet. Powered by rockets, it first flew in 1941.

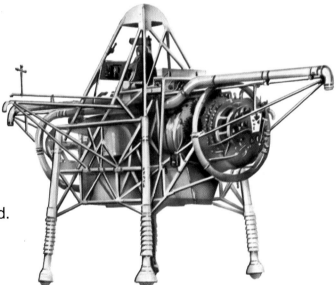

▲ The Flying Bedstead was a British research machine that tested methods of vertical take-off and landing. It could hover in mid-air and move slowly up and down.

Windmills in the Sky

There is another way to hover in the air or to achieve vertical flight. A helicopter has windmill-like rotor blades which allow it to perform any kind of movement in the air that its pilot may wish. These aircraft are used to take people into the centre of cities or out to oil rigs, for example, where there is not enough room for aeroplanes to land. Helicopters are vital for rescue work at sea and in mountains.

How a helicopter works

The whirling rotor blades of a helicopter work like rotating wings and like a propellor. The blades have aerofoil shapes like wings to produce lift as they cut through the air, but they also push air back to move the helicopter. By tilting the rotor in flight, the helicopter can be made to fly forwards or backwards as well as straight up and down.

First flights

The idea of the helicopter is not new. In China, children played with whirling toys that flew up into the air at least 800 years ago. In about 1500, the Italian artist Leonardo da Vinci sketched a helicopter, but it was never made. It could not have flown at that time, because no engine both light and powerful enough for flight existed then.

Model helicopters were flown in the 1800s using steam engines and other sources of power. But machines that could lift a person into the air had, like aeroplanes, to await the petrol engine. The first piloted flights were made in 1907 in France but, unlike aeroplanes, which developed rapidly, it took a long time to perfect helicopters. This was because the mechanism needed to tilt the rotor is very complex, and it was about 30 years before safe controlled flight was achieved.

Meanwhile, another kind of 'whirlybird' took to the air. This was the autogiro, invented by the Spanish engineer Juan de la Cierva in 1923. A propellor drove it through the air, but instead of wings it had an unpowered rotor, like a helicopter. The rotor blades spun round as the autogiro moved forward, lifting the machine into the air.

The first true helicopter appeared in 1936. This was the German twin-rotor Focke-Wulf Fw-61. The American single-rotor Sikorsky VS-300, built by Igor Sikorsky (see page 31), dates from 1939 and was the ancestor of most present-day helicopters, which have a single main rotor and another small tail rotor to prevent the helicopter from spinning out of control.

The first helicopter to make a free (untethered) flight was built in France by Paul Cornu. It first flew in 13 November 1907.

▲ Leonardo da Vinci's sketch of a helicopter design, drawn in about 1500.

Helicopters have rescued many people from ships sinking in violent storms at sea.

The Future

Human flight is just two centuries old. In that time, many different kinds of flying machine – balloons, airships, gliders, aeroplanes with an extraordinary variety of wings and engines, autogiros, helicopters – have risen into the sky. The future is likely to produce a whole new range of aircraft. Helping their development will be new light but super-strong materials to build them, powerful and non-polluting fuels such as hydrogen to drive them, and special computers that will not only produce safe new designs but also fly the aircraft.

Military aircraft

One idea for the fighter of the future is to have wings that are swept forward, unlike today's aircraft which have swept-back wings. They would also have small wings at the front. Such an aircraft would look like a modern fighter with the wings and tail turned round! It could fly very well at both low and high speeds. Control of the wing surfaces would be difficult, so an onboard computer would be needed to help the pilot.

The most amazing design for the future of air travel is this ring-wing aircraft, now undergoing wind-tunnel tests. If these are successful, this aircraft could be gracing the skies in about 2000. ▶

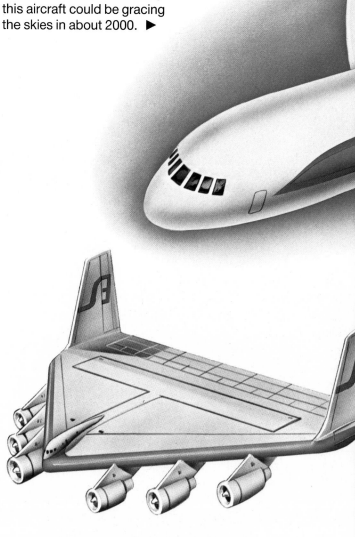

▲ A design for a twin-bodied aircraft of the future produced by NASA and Lockheed in the United States. It would cost less to fly than today's air transports.

▲ Another idea for an energy-saving air transport of the future is this huge Lockheed flying wing that would make today's jumbo jets look tiny by comparison.

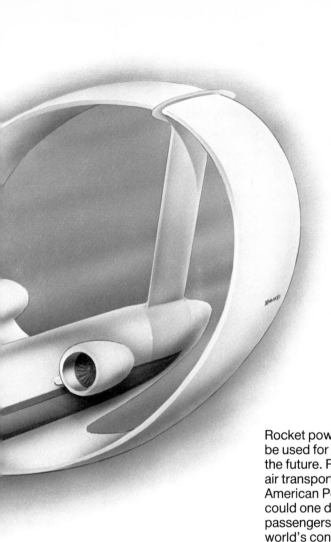

Rocket power may not only be used for space travel in the future. Rocket-powered air transports like this American Pegasus project could one day be whisking passengers across the world's continents and oceans. ▶

Remote control aircraft

In the United States, NASA has tested a half-size fighter of the future called HIMAT (Highly Manoeuvrable Aircraft Technology). HIMAT has no pilot on board. Instead the pilot stays on the ground, flying the aircraft by remote control with the aid of a television camera in the aircraft's nose. HIMAT can test designs which allow the very fast but tight turns that a future fighter plane is likely to perform. To fly in this way, it has wings that twist and bend in flight, extra small wings at the front, fins on the wing tips and twin rudders.

Large military aircraft of the future, which could be flying control centres as well as bombers or missile launches, are likely to have rounded surfaces with special paints that will make them invisible to enemy radar. Aircraft that look like great flying wings may patrol the fringes of space, ready to knock out enemy satellites overhead.

Airliners and freighters

Airliners are unlikely to change very much in looks in the near future, but they should become quieter. Airlines will look for aircraft that are cheap to fly, and one possible design is a large twin-bodied aircraft that would look like two aircraft joined together. Another is a flying wing so enormous that it would dwarf today's jumbo jets.

Strange shapes

Some really unusual aircraft may come to transport the people of the future. A ring-wing airliner, with a circular wing curled right around its body, could be flying in the next century. Other ideas include aircraft combining balloons, rotors and wings. These futuristic flying machines could be used as inexpensive air freighters, and would be large helium-filled airships with sets of rotors or wings to improve performance both high in the air and near the ground.

Books and Places

Books to read
The Guinness Book of Air Facts and Feats, J. W. R. Taylor, J. H. Taylor and D. Mondey, Guinness Superlatives.
Back To The Drawing Board, Allen Andrews, David & Charles, 1977.
Family Library Of Aircraft, Bill Gunston, Octopus, 1982.
Incredible Flying Machines, Michael Jerram, Marshall Cavendish, 1980.
Gliding, Derek Piggott, A & C. Black, 1976.
Ballooning Handbook, Don Cameron, Pelham, 1980.
The Model Aircraft Handbook, Howard G. McEntee, Hale, 1982.
The Penguin Book Of Kites, David Pelham, Penguin, 1976.

Places to visit
The best places to see aircraft in action are **airports**. At international airports, airliners from most countries can be seen taking off or landing.

Military aircraft may be seen at air-force bases, but you should take care in these places. Remember, too, that taking photographs may be forbidden.

Air shows are good events at which to see both new and historic aircraft. These shows take place at airfields in many places, generally during the summer, and may include displays of aerobatics, formation flying, sky diving and parachute jumping. The best-known air show in Britain takes place at Farnborough, Hampshire, every other year.

The British pilot Amy Johnson was the first woman to fly solo from Britain to Australia. ▼

Air museums exhibit historic planes, some of which may still be in flying condition. In addition to these, you may also see replicas of famous aircraft. In Britain, for example, the following museums display famous aircraft:

The Science Museum, South Kensington, London, SW7; The Imperial War Museum, Lambeth, London, SE1; The RAF Museum and Battle of Britain Museum, Hendon, London SW9; The Shuttleworth Collection, Old Warden, Biggleswade, Bedfordshire; Imperial War Museum Collection, Duxford, Cambridgeshire; Aerospace Museum, Gosford, Wolverhampton, West Midlands; Fleet Air Arm Museum, Yeovilton, Somerset.

In Europe, there is the Musée National Des Techniques (Conservatoire National Des Arts Et Métiers), Paris, France. In this museum, you can see a steam-powered, bat-winged aircraft built by Clément Ader in 1897, the monoplane in which Louis Blériot made the first crossing of the English Channel in 1909, and a very early helicopter of 1905. An important science museum with a good display of aircraft is the Deutsches Museum, Munich, West Germany.

In the National Air And Space Museum, Washington DC, USA, you can see the world's first aeroplane, the Wright brothers' Flyer 1; Spirit of St. Louis, the plane in which Lindbergh made the first solo transatlantic crossing, and the Bell XS-1, the first supersonic aircraft.

Pioneer of Flight

Alcock, Sir John (1892–1919) and **Brown, Sir Arthur** (1886–1948) were two British airmen who made the first non-stop flight across the Atlantic Ocean in 1919. They flew in a Vickers Vimy twin-engined biplane bomber from Newfoundland to Ireland, taking 16 hours 12 minutes. Alcock was the pilot and Brown the navigator.
Blériot, Louis (1872–1936) was a French airman who made the first aeroplane flight across the English Channel on 31 October 1909 in his monoplane.
Byrd, Richard (1888–1957) was a United States airman who made the first flight over the North Pole on 9 May 1926 and then the first flight over the South Pole on 28–29 November 1929 in a Fokker FVII monoplane.

Cayley, Sir George
(1773–1857) was a British engineer who was the first person to discover how aircraft could fly. He established the basic design of wings and a tail fitted to a long body with his model glider of 1804, which was the first real aeroplane. Cayley built the first glider to carry a person aloft, sending a boy up in a glider in 1849.

Charles, Jacques
(1746–1823) was a French scientist who, accompanied by M. Robert, made the first flight in a hydrogen-filled balloon over Paris on 1 December 1783.

Cody, Samuel (1861–1913) was an American airman who lived in Britain. He designed and flew people-lifting kites and then built and flew the first British airship, Nulli Secundus, in 1907. Cody made the first official aeroplane flight in Britain on 16 October 1908 in the British Army Aeroplane No 1. The flight covered 424 metres.

Johnson, Amy (1903–1941) was a British pilot who was the first woman to fly solo from Britain to Australia. Her flight, in a De Havilland Gipsy Moth, took ten days from 5 to 14 May 1930.

Lilienthal, Otto
(1848–1896) was a German airman who made and flew the first practical gliders. His designs for monoplane hang-gliders led to the first powered aircraft.

Lindbergh, Charles
(1902–1974) was a United States airman who, in 1927, made the first solo non-stop flight across the Atlantic Ocean. Lindbergh flew in a Ryan monoplane called Spirit of St Louis, taking 33½ hours to fly from New York to Paris.

Montgolfier, Joseph
(1740–1810) and **Etienne**
(1745–1799) were two French brothers who built the first balloon to carry people aloft. The balloon, a hot-air balloon, flew 8 kilometres over Paris on 21 November 1783.

Santos-Dumont, Alberto
(1873–1932) was a Brazilian airman who lived in France. In 1898, he built an airship that was so easy to fly that he would land in the streets of Paris to meet people. In 1901, he won a prize of 100,000 francs by flying it around the Eiffel Tower. He later made the first powered aeroplane flight in Europe in 1906, flying his own 14-bis.

Wright, Wilbur (1867–1912) and **Orville** (1871–1948) were two United States brothers who made the first powered aeroplane flight on 17 December 1903 with their own aircraft Flyer 1. Orville Wright made the very first flight. The Wright brothers began building successful gliders in 1899 and led the world in aeroplane design for many years. Their Flyer 3 of 1905 was the first practical aeroplane able to bank and turn. In 1908, this became the first passenger aircraft when Orville Wright took a friend aloft.

▲ Formation flying by teams such as the Red Arrows thrills people at air shows.

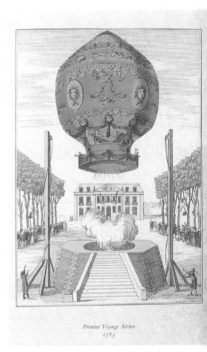

Premier Voyage Aérien
1783

▲ The Montgolfier hot-air balloon making the first free balloon ascent with people aboard, on 21 November 1783.

Word list

Aerobatics A display of thrilling manoeuvres, such as flying in a loop and rolling, twisting and diving in unusual ways.

Aerofoil The curved shape of a wing that is seen if you look at the wing from the wingtip. It curves upward and is thickest near the middle. A wing must have an aerofoil shape to fly.

Aeroplane An aircraft that has wings and an engine. An aeroplane is called an airplane in the U.S.A.

Aircraft Any kind of flying machine, including aeroplanes, gliders and helicopters.

Airline A company or an organization that operates air transport services.

Airliner An aeroplane that carries passengers or freight.

Airplane The same as aeroplane.

Airship An aircraft intended to carry passengers or freight that is lighter than air. It consists of a large balloon to which a cabin and engines are attached. The largest airships were much bigger than today's airliners.

Biplane An aeroplane with two pairs of wings, one above the other.

Control surfaces The main wings and tailplane of an aeroplane and a glider have flaps along the back edges. These flaps are called control surfaces as they help control the aircraft's flight. Raising the flaps on the tailplane makes the nose of the aircraft rise, and lowering them makes it dip. Raising a back flap on one wing while lowering that of the other makes the aeroplane tilt when turning. Other flaps on the wings are extended during take-off and landing to increase lift.

Envelope The large round canopy of a balloon that contains the hot air or light gas.

Glider An aircraft with wings but without an engine.

Helium The second lightest gas. It is found mixed in small amounts with natural gas.

Hummingbirds A group of small brightly-coloured birds that live in South, Central and North America. Hummingbirds get their name because they can beat their wings so quickly that they make a humming sound.

Hydrogen The lightest gas of all. Hydrogen is not found as a gas, but is made when an electric current is passed through water.

Lift The force that holds an aircraft up in the air. The wings of an aeroplane and the main rotor of a helicopter produce lift. So too does the envelope of a balloon, when it is filled with lighter-than-air gases. When the force of the lift is equal to the weight of the aircraft, it flies at the same height or hovers in the air. If the lift is greater than the weight, the aircraft rises. If the lift is less, it descends.

Mach Number (pronounced *mark number*) A measure of the speed of an aircraft. Mach 1 is the speed of sound, Mach 2 twice the speed of sound and so on.

Manoeuvre A sharp turn, twist or roll in flight.

Migration A long journey made by an animal, usually twice every year. The animal migrates from the region in which it breeds to another region where food can be found, and then migrates back to breed once more. Many, but not all, birds migrate, and so do some land and sea animals.

Monoplane An aeroplane with one pair of wings, one on either side of its body.

Rudder A flap on the vertical tailfin of an aeroplane or glider which is turned to make the aircraft change direction.

Runway A long level stretch of ground, generally paved, that is used by aeroplanes and gliders to take off and land. The runway at an international airport may be as long as five kilometres.

Soaring The kind of flight made by a bird in which it stretches out its wings and glides through the air without flapping them. Gliders also soar.

Sound Barrier When an aircraft reaches a speed faster than the speed at which sound travels, we say that it goes through the Sound Barrier. When this happens, a bang is heard on the ground below the aircraft.

Stall If an aircraft stalls, it loses lift and begins to fall out of control. This can happen if it flies too slowly or raises its nose too high. A good pilot can recover from a stall and regain control.

Supersonic An aircraft that can fly faster than the speed of sound is said to be supersonic. Supersonic flight is flight at speeds faster than sound. Concorde, the most famous supersonic aircraft, can fly over twice as fast as the speed of sound.

Triplane An old kind of aircraft which has three pairs of wings mounted one above the other.

Index